Aeschylus
Quotes & Facts

By Blago Kirov

First Edition

D1636623

*****

Aeschylus: Quotes & Facts
*****

Copyright © 2016 by Blago Kirov

Foreword

"The words of truth are simple."

This book is an anthology of quotes from Aeschylus and selected facts about Aeschylus.

"A great ox stands on my tongue."
"A prosperous fool is a grievous burden."
"Against necessity, against its strength, no one can fight and win."
"Ask the gods nothing excessive."
"Be bold and boast, just like the cock beside the hen."
"Bronze is the mirror of the form; wine, of the heart."
"But time growing old teaches all things."
"By polluting clear water with slime you will never find good drinking water."
"Call no man happy till he is dead."
"Do not kick against the pricks."
"Every ruler is harsh whose rule is new."
"Fear is stronger than arms."
"For hostile word let hostile word be paid."
"For know that no one is free, except Zeus."
"For the mighty even to give way is grace."
"From a small seed a mighty trunk may grow."
"God loves to help him who strives to help himself."
"Happiness is a choice that requires effort at times."
"I say you must not win an unjust case by oaths."
"I'm not afraid of storms, for I'm learning to sail my ship."
"In war, truth is the first casualty."
"It is not the oath that makes us believe the man, but the man the oath."
"It is the nature of mortals to kick a fallen man."
"Married love between man and woman is bigger than oaths guarded by right of nature."

"Memory is the mother of all wisdom."
"Obedience is the mother of success and is wedded to safety."
"Only when a man's life comes to its end in prosperity dare we pronounce him happy."
"The words of truth are simple."

Some Facts about Aeschylus

Aeschylus (c. 525/524 – c. 456/455 BC) was an ancient Greek tragedian.

Aeschylus was born in c. 525 BC in Eleusis, a small town about 27 kilometers northwest of Athens, which is nestled in the fertile valleys of western Attica, though the date is most likely based on counting back forty years from his first victory in the Great Dionysia.

His family was wealthy and well established; his father, Euphorion, was a member of the Eupatridae, the ancient nobility of Attica, though this might be a fiction that the ancients invented to account for the grandeur of his plays.

As a youth, he worked at a vineyard until, according to the 2nd-century AD geographer Pausanias, the god Dionysus visited him in his sleep and commanded him to turn his attention to the nascent art of tragedy.

His first performance took place in 499 BC, when he was only 26 years old.

He would win his first victory at the City Dionysia in 484 BC.

In 510 BC, when Aeschylus was 15 years old, Cleomenes I expelled the sons of Peisistratus from Athens, and Cleisthenes came to power.

In 490 BC, Aeschylus and his brother Cynegeirus fought to defend Athens against Darius I's invading Persian army at the Battle of Marathon.

In 480, Aeschylus was called into military service again, this time against Xerxes I's invading forces at the Battle of Salamis, and perhaps, too, at the Battle of Plataea in 479.

Ion of Chios was a witness for Aeschylus's war record and his contribution in Salamis.

Salamis holds a prominent place in The Persians, his oldest surviving play, which was performed in 472 BC and won first prize at the Dionysia.

Aeschylus was one of many Greeks who had been initiated into the Eleusinian Mysteries, a cult to Demeter based in his hometown of Eleusis.

According to Aristotle some thought that Aeschylus had revealed some of the cult's secrets on stage.

Aeschylus travelled to Sicily once or twice in the 470s BC, having been invited by Hiero I of Syracuse, a major Greek city on the eastern side of the island; and during one of these trips he produced The Women of Aetna (in honor of the city founded by Hieron) and restaged his Persians.

By 473 BC, after the death of Phrynichus, one of his chief rivals, Aeschylus was the yearly favorite in the Dionysia, winning first prize in nearly every competition.

In 472 BC, Aeschylus staged the production that included the Persians, with Pericles serving as choregos.

In 458 BC, he returned to Sicily for the last time, visiting the city of Gela where he died in 456 or 455 BC.

Valerius Maximus wrote that he was killed outside the city by a tortoise dropped by an eagle which had mistaken his head for a rock suitable for shattering the shell of the reptile.

Aeschylus's work was so respected by the Athenians that after his death, his were the only tragedies allowed to be restaged in subsequent competitions.

His sons Euphorion and Euæon and his nephew Philocles also became playwrights.

Euphorion won first prize in 431 in competition against both Sophocles and Euripides.

His nephew, Philocles (his sister's son), was also a tragic poet, and won first prize in the competition against Sophocles' Oedipus Rex.

Aeschylus had at least two brothers, Cynegeirus and Ameinias.

Only seven of his tragedies have survived intact: The Persians, Seven against Thebes, The Suppliants, the trilogy known as The Oresteia, consisting of the three tragedies Agamemnon, The Libation Bearers and The Eumenides, together with Prometheus Bound (whose authorship is disputed).

The Alexandrian Life of Aeschylus claims that he won the first prize at the City Dionysia thirteen times.

One hallmark of Aeschylean dramaturgy appears to have been his tendency to write connected trilogies, in which each play serves as a chapter in a continuous dramatic narrative. The Oresteia is the only extant example of this type of connected trilogy, but there is evidence that Aeschylus often wrote such trilogies.

Scholars have moreover suggested several completely lost trilogies derived from known play titles. A number of these trilogies treated myths surrounding the Trojan War.

The earliest of his plays to survive is The Persians (Persai), performed in 472 BC and based on experiences in Aeschylus's own life, specifically the Battle of Salamis.

Seven against Thebes (Hepta epi Thebas), which was performed in 467 BC, has the contrasting theme of the interference of the gods in human affairs. It also marks the first known appearance in Aeschylus's work of a theme which would continue through his plays, that of the polis (the city) being a key development of human civilization.

Aeschylus continued his emphasis on the polis with The Suppliants in 463 BC (Hiketides), which pays tribute to the democratic undercurrents running through Athens in advance of the establishment of a democratic government in 461.

The only complete (save a few missing lines in several spots) trilogy of Greek plays by any playwright still extant is the Oresteia (458 BC). The trilogy consists of Agamemnon, The Libation Bearers (Choephoroi), and The Eumenides. Together, these plays tell the bloody story of the family of Agamemnon, King of Argos.

Only the titles and assorted fragments of Aeschylus's other plays have come down to us. These are the remaining 71 plays ascribed to Aeschylus which are known.

When Aeschylus first began writing, the theatre had only just begun to evolve.

Aeschylus added a second actor, allowing for greater dramatic variety, while the chorus played a less important role.

He is sometimes credited with introducing skenographia, or scene-decoration, though Aristotle gives this distinction to Sophocles.

Aeschylus is also said to have made the costumes more elaborate and dramatic, and having his actors wear platform boots (cothurni) to make them more visible to the audience.

According to a later account of Aeschylus's life, as they walked on stage in the first performance of the Eumenides, the chorus of Furies were so frightening in appearance that they caused young children to faint, patriarchs to urinate, and pregnant women to go into labour.

His plays were written in verse, no violence is performed on stage, and the plays have a remoteness from daily life in Athens, either by relating stories about the gods or by being set, like The Persians, in far-away locales.

Aeschylus's works were influential beyond his own time. Hugh Lloyd-Jones draws attention to Richard Wagner's reverence of Aeschylus.

His Aeschylus and Sophocles: Their Work and Influence that Aeschylus, along with Sophocles, have played a major part in the formation of dramatic literature from the Renaissance to the present, specifically in French and Elizabethan drama.

His Words

"A god implants in mortal guilt whenever he wants
utterly to confound a house."

"A great ox stands on my tongue."

"A prosperous fool is a grievous burden."

"Against necessity, against its strength, no one can fight and win."

"Alas for the affairs of men! When they are fortunate you might compare them to a shadow; and if they are unfortunate, a wet sponge with one dash wipes the picture away."

"And one who is just of his own free will shall not lack for happiness; and he will never come to utter ruin."

"And though all streams flow from a single course to cleanse the blood from polluted hand, they hasten on their course in vain."

"Ask the gods nothing excessive."

"Be bold and boast, just like the cock beside the hen."

"Be it mine to draw from wisdom's fount, pure as it flows, that calm of soul which virtue only knows."

"Beyond age, leaf withered, man goes three footed no stronger than a child is, a dream that falters in daylight."

"Bronze is the mirror of the form; wine, of the heart."

"But time growing old teaches all things."

"By polluting clear water with slime you will never find good drinking water."

"By Time and Age full many things are taught."

"Call no man happy till he is dead."

"Death is better, a milder fate than tyranny."

"Death is easier than a wretched life; and better never to have born than to live and fare badly."

"Destiny waits alike for the free man as well as for him enslaved by another's might."

"Do not kick against the pricks."

"Do you not know, Prometheus, that words are healers of the sick temper?"

"Don't you know this, that words are doctors to a diseased temperament?"

"Drop, drop in our sleep, upon the heart sorrow falls, memory's pain, and to us, though against our very will,even in our own despite, comes wisdom by the awful grace of God."

"Every ruler is harsh whose rule is new."

"Everyone's quick to blame the alien."

"Excessive fear is always powerless."

"Fear is stronger than arms."

"For a deadly blow let him pay with a deadly blow; it is for him who has done a deed to suffer."

"For children preserve the fame of a man after his death."

"For hostile word let hostile word be paid."

"For know that no one is free, except Zeus."

"For somehow this disease inheres in tyranny, never to trust one's friends."

"For sufferers it is sweet to know before-hand clearly the pain that still remains for them."

"For the impious act begets more after it, like to the parent stock."

"For the mighty even to give way is grace."

"For the poison of hatred seated near the heart doubles the burden for the one who suffers the disease; he is burdened with his own sorrow, and groans on seeing another's happiness."

"For there is no defense for a man who, in the excess of his wealth, has kicked the great altar of Justice out of sight."

"For this is the mark of a wise and upright man, not to rail against the gods in misfortune."

"From a small seed a mighty trunk may grow."

"God always strives together with those who strive."

"God loves to help him who strives to help himself."

"God's most lordly gift to man is decency of mind."

"God's mouth knows not how to speak falsehood, but he brings to pass every word."

"Good fortune is a god among men, and more than a god."

"Happiness is a choice that requires effort at times."

"He who goes unenvied shall not be admired."

"He who learns must suffer. And even in our sleep pain that cannot forget falls drop by drop upon the heart, and in our own despair, against our will, comes wisdom to us by the awful grace of God."

"His resolve is not to seem, but to be, the best."

"Hold him alone truly fortunate who has ended his life in happy well-being."

"Human prosperity never rests but always craves more, till blown up with pride it totters and falls. From the opulent mansions pointed at by all passers-by none warns it away, none cries, Let no more riches enter!"

"I have learned to hate all traitors, and there is no disease that I spit on more than treachery."

"I know how men in exile feed on dreams of hope."

"I pray for no more youth to perish before its prime That Revenge and iron-heated War May fade with all that has gone before Into the night of time."

"I say you must not win an unjust case by oaths."

"I willingly speak to those who know, but for those who do not know I forget."

"I would far rather be ignorant than knowledgeable of evil."

"I, schooled in misery, know many purifying rites, and I know where speech is proper and where silence."

"If a man suffers ill, let it be without shame; for this is the only profit when we are dead. You will never say a good word about deeds that are evil and disgraceful."

"If you pour oil and vinegar into the same vessel, you would call them not friends but opponents."

"I'm not afraid of storms, for I'm learning to sail my ship."

"In every tyrant's heart there springs in the end this poison, that he cannot trust a friend."

"In few men is it part of nature to respect a friend's prosperity without begrudging him."

"In the lack of judgment great harm arises, but one vote cast can set right a house."

"In war, truth is the first casualty."

"Innumerable twinkling of the waves of the sea."

"It is a light thing for whoever keeps his foot outside trouble to advise and counsel him that suffers."

"It is a profitable thing, if one is wise, to seem foolish."

"It is an easy thing for one whose foot is on the outside of calamity to give advice and to rebuke the sufferer."

"It is an ill thing to be the first to bring news of ill."

"It is easy when we are in prosperity to give advice to the afflicted."

"It is good even for old men to learn wisdom."

"It is in the character of very few men to honor without envy a friend who has prospered."

"It is not the oath that makes us believe the man, but the man the oath."

"It is the nature of mortals to kick a fallen man."

"Justice turns the scale, bringing to some learning through suffering."

"Know not to revere human things too much."

"Learning is ever in the freshness of its youth, even for the old."

"Let there be wealth without tears; enough for the wise man who will ask no further."

"Many among men are they who set high the show of honor, yet break justice."

"Married love between man and woman is bigger than oaths guarded by right of nature."

"Memory is the mother of all wisdom."

"Misfortune wandering the same track lights now upon one and now upon another."

"Mourn for me rather as living than as dead."

"My friends, whoever has had experience of evils knows how whenever a flood of ills comes upon mortals, a man fears everything; but whenever a divine force cheers on our voyage, then we believe that the same fate will always blow fair."

"Neither a life of anarchy nor one beneath a despot should you praise; to all that lies in the middle a god has given excellence."

"O Death the Healer, scorn thou not, I pray, To come to me: of cureless ills thou art The one physician. Pain lays not its touch Upon a corpse."

"Obedience is the mother of success and is wedded to safety."

"Obstinacy standing alone is the weakest of all things in one whose mind is not possessed by wisdom."

"Of all the gods, Death only craves not gifts: Nor sacrifice, nor yet drink-offering poured Avails; no altars hath he, nor is soothed By hymns of praise. From him alone of all The powers of heaven Persuasion holds aloof."

"Of prosperity mortals can never have enough."

"Oh me, I have been struck a mortal blow right inside."

"On me the tempest falls. It does not make me tremble. O holy Mother Earth, O air and sun, behold me. I am wronged."

"Only when a man's life comes to its end in prosperity dare we pronounce him happy."

"Reverence for parents stands written among the three laws of most revered righteousness."

"Search well and be wise, nor believe that self-willed pride will ever be better than good counsel."

"Self-will in the man who does not reckon wisely is by itself the weakest of all things."

"She brought to Ilium her dowry, destruction."

"Since long I've held silence a remedy for harm."

"So in the Libyan fable it is told That once an eagle, stricken with a dart, Said, when he saw the fashion of the shaft, With our own feathers, not by others' hands, Are we now smitten."

"Success! to thee, as to a God, men bend the knee."

"The act of evil breeds others to follow, young sins in its own likeness."

"The anvil of justice is planted firm, and fate who makes the sword does the forging in advance."

"The evils of mortals are manifold; nowhere is trouble of the same wing seen."

"The future you shall know when it has come; before then, forget it."

"The high strength of men knows no content with limitation."

"The man who does ill must suffer ill."

"The man whose authority is recent is always stern."

"The misfortunes of mankind are of varied plumage."

"The one knowing what is profitable, and not the man knowing many things, is wise."

"The power that holds the sky's majesty wins our worship."

"The tongue of slander is too prompt with wanton malice to wound the stranger."

"The wisest of the wise may err."

"The words of truth are simple."

"There are times when fear is good. It must keep its watchful place at the heart's controls. There is advantage in the wisdom won from pain."

"There is no disgrace in an enemy suffering ill at an enemy's hand, when you hate mutually."

"There is no pain so great as the memory of joy in present grief."

"There is no sickness worse for me than words that to be kind must lie."

"There's nothing certain in a man's life except this: That he must lose it."

"They who prosper take on airs of vanity."

"This is a sickness rooted and inherent in the nature of a tyranny: that he that holds it does not trust his friends."

"Time as he grows old teaches all things."

"Time brings all things to pass."

"To be fortunate is God, and more than God to mortals."

"To be free from evil thoughts is God's best gift."

"To mourn and bewail your ill-fortune, when you will gain a tear from those who listen, this is worth the trouble."

"To the man who himself strives earnestly, God also lends a helping hand."

"Too few rejoice at a friend's good fortune."

"Unions in wedlock are perverted by the victory of shameless passion that masters the female among men and beasts."

"We must pronounce him fortunate who has ended his life in fair prosperity."

"We shall perish by guile just as we slew."

"What atonement is there for blood spilt upon the earth?"

"What exists outside is a man's concern; let no woman give advice; and do no mischief within doors."

"What good is it to live a life that brings pains?"

"What is there more kindly than the feeling between host and guest?"

"When a match has equal partners then I fear not."

"When one is willing and eager, the Gods join in."

"When strength is yoked with justice, where is a mightier pair than they?"

"Whenever a man makes haste, God too hastens with him."

"Who apart from the gods is without pain for his whole lifetime's length?"

"Who holds a power but newly gained is ever stern of mood."

"Who, except the gods, can live time through forever
without any pain?"

"Whoever is new to power is always harsh."

"Wisdom comes through suffering. Trouble, with its
memories of pain, Drips in our hearts as we try to
sleep, So men against their will Learn to practice
moderation. Favours come to us from gods."

"Words are the physicians of a mind diseased."

"Wrong must not win by technicalities."

"You have been trapped in the inescapable net of ruin
by your own want of sense."

"Zeus, first cause, prime mover; for what thing without
Zeus is done among mortals?"

38248023R00019

Made in the USA
Middletown, DE
15 December 2016